T0035047

For the ghosts.

Thank you to David Clarke, Hayley Stevens and
Philippe Baudouin for their occult expertise.

Tremendous gratitude to the Flying Eye elves
for their wisdom and hard work.

Also in the series:

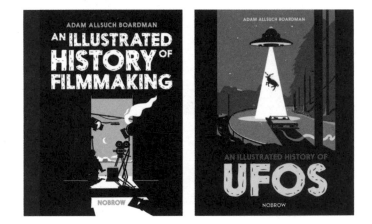

First edition published in 2022 by Flying Eye Books Ltd.
27 Westgate Street, London E8 3RL.

Text and illustrations © Adam Allsuch Boardman 2022

Consultants: Dr David Clarke and Hayley Stevens

Adam Allsuch Boardman has asserted his right under the Copyright, Designs
and Patents Act, 1988, to be identified as the Author and Illustrator of this Work.

All rights reserved. No part of this publication may be reproduced or transmitted in any form or
by any means, electronic or mechanical, including photocopying, recording or by any information
and storage retrieval system, without prior written consent from the publisher.

10 9 8 7 6 5 4 3 2

Published in the US by Flying Eye Books Ltd.
Printed in Poland on FSC® certified paper.

MIX
Paper from
responsible sources
FSC® C163799

ISBN: 978-1-913123-07-9

www.flyingeyebooks.com

ADAM ALLSUCH BOARDMAN

AN ILLUSTRATED HISTORY OF
GHOSTS

FLYING EYE BOOKS

CONTENTS

Ever since we first committed words to tablet, there have been recorded dalliances with ghosts. They come in all shapes and sizes, such as gloomy grey ladies and creeping nightmares.

They haunt our stories, from Gilgamesh's beloved Enkidu to Peter Venkman's messy encounter with Slimer in *Ghostbusters* (1984).

But why do people believe in ghosts? For some it is a matter of tradition as ghosts have emerged from myths and legends. Belief can also be cultivated by the inexplicable. For every mysterious bump heard and apparition glimpsed, there begins a potential ghost sighting.

And the hunt for ghosts has spawned a plethora of blinking gadgets, theories and tourist hotspots. Intrepid investigators and scene-stealing mediums have forayed where many feared to tread and have visited haunted castles, graveyards and far-flung forests.

This book has collected many myths, legends and curiosities surrounding the phenomena of ghosts. I hope you'll read further, or even try a spot of ghost hunting yourself, with a torch and a hot drink in hand.

WHAT IS A GHOST?

Ghosts are thought to be spirits of the dead that often lurk near places important to their former lives. Etymologically, the word ghost comes from the Germanic word *gást* meaning soul or spirit.

Throughout time, many people have reported ghost sightings. Encounters range from fleeting glimpses of glowing ghouls to spectral ships on stormy seas. Besides contemporary accounts, ghosts are relayed through myths and legends.

Legend
Legends are stories about people and places that may or may not be authentic but are often believed by an audience.

Myth
Myths are stories tied strongly to a belief system, such as the Bible or ancient Greek mythos. Myths can take thousands of years to develop and are often used to explain mysterious phenomena.

Types of Ghosts

The exact characteristics of ghosts can be confusing due to many cultural interpretations and definitions. English researcher, Peter Underwood, organised ghosts and related spirits into neat groups:

Elementals
A broad spectrum of nature spirits, such as faeries, goblins and demons.

Poltergeists
In German this word means noisy ghost. These ghosts are theatrical in nature and enjoy throwing objects around.

Traditional Ghosts
Spirits of the dead that are restless and sometimes talkative.

Mental Imprints
Apparitions left in the material world by historic events.

Crisis and Death-Survival Apparitions
Apparitions seen by the friends and family of someone who is close to death.

Time Slips
Localised time travel ghosts, such as the sudden appearance of an historic scene.

Ghosts of the Living
Mental projections by psychic people.

Haunted Inanimate Objects
Objects and vehicles that exhibit ghostly activity.

WHAT IS A HAUNTING?

When ghosts are believed to dwell in a fixed place it is called a haunting. Traditionally, it is thought ghosts haunt the sites of their deaths, or places that were important during their lives.

People have witnessed many strange phenomena which they have attributed to a haunting.

1. **Apparition**
   A full or partial ghostly figure is seen.

2. **Apporting**
   The sudden appearance of objects.

3. **Electrical Interference**
   Lights dimming, and appliances acting oddly.

4. **Ghost Writing**
   Written messages on walls and mirrors.

5. **Knocking and Footsteps**
Commonplace sounds with unknown origins.

6. **Peculiar Pets**
The odd behaviour of animals, such as a dog barking at an empty corner

7. **Phantom Music**
The sound of music from an unseen source.

8. **Voices from the Void**
Indistinct whisperings and disembodied conversations.

9. **Cold Spots**
The unusual coldness of a room.

10. **Phantom Stains**
The appearance of stains or marks.

11. **Anomalous Injuries**
Bumps, bruises and scratches have been reported as poltergeist activity.

12. **Levitation**
Objects that seem to float or move under their own volition.

13. **Possession**
A person or object inhabited by an invasive sprit.

14. **High Strangeness**
Dreamlike encounters.

SCEPTICAL INQUIRY

When evidence for paranormal claims is studied in detail, rather than accepted on faith, it is called sceptical inquiry. Throughout history, self-styled sceptics have investigated reputed hauntings to provide scientific explanations.

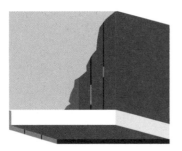

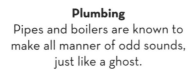

Wonky Foundations
Buildings with foundational damage can shake and make strange noises.

Plumbing
Pipes and boilers are known to make all manner of odd sounds, just like a ghost.

Hoaxing
People fake hauntings for various reasons. These can range from amusement to the pursuit of profit.

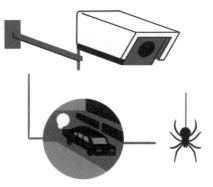

Hallucinations
These may be caused by head injuries and mental illnesses.

Creepy-Crawlies
Spiders, flies and other small creatures are sometimes mistaken for ghosts when they crawl over camera equipment.

Optical Illusions
Tricks of light and shadow that appear as ghosts.

Infrasound
Some studies have shown that low frequency sounds can lead to unease, dizziness and nausea.

Pareidolia
When a person sees random patterns in unrelated objects and assigns them with meaning.

Sleep Paralysis
A dreamlike awakening during sleep. A person can feel a weight on their chest and experience hallucinations.

Confirmation Bias
A pre-existing belief in the paranormal may lead witnesses to ignore other explanations.

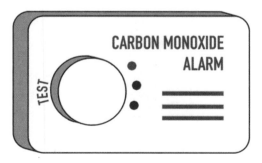

Carbon Monoxide (CO)
Exposure to this poisonous gas can cause dizziness and hallucinations.

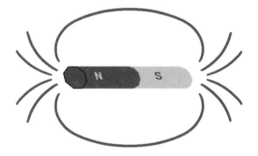

Electro Magnetic Field (EMF)
EMF's effects on humans are strongly disputed. Some believe high levels of EMF create a sense of unease and disorientation.

PREMODERNITY

Oldest picture of a ghost, Babylonian clay tablet (circa 1500 BCE)

AFTERLIFE

In many ancient mythologies, ghosts were believed to be souls of the dead which had eluded the afterlife. Tradition taught that careful burial practices aided souls on their afterlife journey. The oldest burial sites discovered are over 10,000 years old. Here ancient people entombed dead bodies in caves with personal items and food.

Wrapped Up

To ancient Egyptians, the body and soul remained linked after death. To aid afterlife activities, they stocked tombs with food and tools. Affluent Egyptians preserved their dead through mummification. This process involved the removal of internal organs and the use of ointments and wrappings to delay decomposition.

Underworld

The ancient Greeks believed spirits of the dead or *shade* were echoes of their mortal form. They buried their dead with coins to secure passage with the underworld's ferryman. It was believed that an unappeased ferryman left souls stranded, causing them to haunt the living.

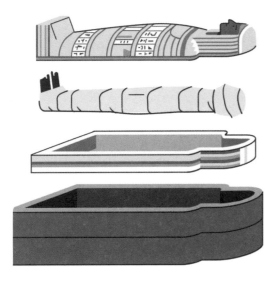

Mummy of the Theban priest Usirmose

Psychopomps

In Aztec mythology, the god Xolotl helped lead ghosts to one of several underworlds. A figure that performs this task is called a psychopomp (Greek for spirit conductor). Aztecs associated Xolotl with the ancient dog breed xoloitzcuintli. Sacrificial dogs and sculptural stand-ins were buried alongside owners to aid in their afterlife journeys.

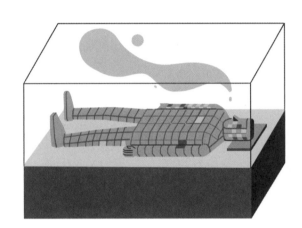

Sections of Soul

In ancient China, it was believed the soul was composed of two parts, the *hun* (cloud soul) and *po* (white-soul). The hun was believed to depart the body upon death, while the po resided in the corpse. During the Han Dynasty (circa 202 BCE–220 CE) nobles were buried in jade suits in effort to preserve their po soul.

Inhabitants of limbo as imagined by renaissance artists.

Limbo

In Catholic theology, limbo (from the medieval Latin for border) is home to dead sinners. It was believed souls could freely wander out of limbo and appear on earth as ghosts. In medieval Europe, the Church sold coupons to those who wanted to avoid assignment to limbo.

HANTU

The Malay peoples in Indonesia, Malaysia and neighbouring regions have developed many myths about ghosts, which they call *Hantu*. Hantu are believed to be receptive to negotiation via rituals and offerings. In some cases, a ghost's services may even be bought.

Bomoh
For a fee, spirit experts called *Bomoh* specialise in negotiating with ghosts in order to cure or inflict sickness.

Pontianak
The ghost of a woman who has died in childbirth.

Toyol
The spirit of an infant child. It was believed that *toyol* could be commissioned to commit petty theft.

Hantu Tetek
A hag-like ghost that is thought to abduct children and return them largely unharmed.

Hantu Jamuan
Party-crashing ghosts that are mischievous until appeased with a meal.

Hantu Kembung
Ghosts that cause headaches and stomach pains, associated with rainy weather.

DUPPY

In the Caribbean, restless ghosts are called *duppy*. The belief in duppy traces from West Africa, and they are thought to take many forms, both human and animal-like. According to legend, duppy are tricksters, capable of causing injury or even death. There are several traditional methods that are thought to thwart the duppy, including wearing clothes inside out, eating salt and offering rum to graves.

Rollin' Calf
The large ghost of a wicked person, commonly described to be cow-like with smoking nostrils and red eyes.

Whooping Boy
A red-eyed child duppy with lethally hot breath.

Birds, Snakes and Lizards
In some cases, duppy take the form of familiar animals.

River Mumma
An aquatic duppy that lures people into perilous waters.

GHOSTLY GUESTS

In some cultures, groups of ghosts make frequent visitations to the material world. This is considered a bad omen by some cultures while others welcome their ghostly guests through festivals.

La Santa Compaña

Since ancient times, people in Portugal and Spain have witnessed a legendary procession of ghosts known as *La Santa Compaña* (The Holy Company). The company wear white hoods to conceal their skeletal features and are led by an entranced mortal from the local area. This mortal is said to awake the next day with no memory of their macabre march.

Tradition dictates that there are a few ways to avoid conscription to the procession, including the drawing of protective symbols or the offering of a black cat (no cats are harmed, thankfully).

Wild Hunt

The apparition known as the Wild Hunt or Ghost Riders appear in legends around the world. These gangs of airborne ghosts are said to ride spectral or flaming horses.

Ghost Festivals

Ghost festivals have been celebrated in countries such as China, Malaysia and Vietnam since the distant past. In Taoism, the event is called the *Zhongyuan Festival* and takes place on the 15th day of the seventh lunar month. The festival has origins in the ancient Buddhist belief that ancestral ghosts ascend from the underworld on an annual basis. During this period, believers welcome the dead with a range of customs.

Ghost King

A large effigy of the King of Ghosts is central to many observances. The effigy is traditionally set alight following the presentation of offerings, the lighting of candles and the burning of incense.

Front Row Seats

During the festivities seats are reserved at live events for the invisible dead to occupy. It is considered very unlucky for living attendees to occupy the seats.

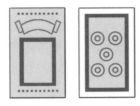

Joss Paper

Special paper called joss paper is burned as an offering to the dead. Joss paper is often decorated with seals, stamps or made to resemble money.

Sights, Sounds and Smells

Incense, lanterns and monastic singing are used in an effort to guide ghosts along streets and rivers.

SEASONAL CELEBRATIONS

Two of the most famous celebrations of the dead, Halloween and *Día de los Muertos* take place at a similar time of the year. This is because their modern incarnations developed from the Catholic All Saints and All Souls Day. Despite this connection, each festival has distinct traditions and can trace their inspiration from unique pre-Christian festivals.

Día de los Muertos

The Mexican Day of the Dead or *Día de los Muertos* is celebrated on the 1st and 2nd of November. Some also believe it might have developed from old Aztec celebrations. The intent of the festival is to honour the dead with revelry, food and attractive decorations.

Look of the Dead

Calavera are decorative depictions of skulls. They appear in sugary snacks, face-paint and as the décor for altars. Historians trace their aesthetic lineage to a fusion of Mesoamerican and European practices. Contemporary designs are highly influenced by the work of 19th century Mexican illustrator José Guadalupe Posada Aguilar.

Ofrendas

Altars called *ofrendas* are decorated with food and bright petals to attract wandering ghosts. It is thought that pleasant and familiar odours attract souls from their graves and into the homes of their friends and families.

Halloween

Halloween was originally a European festival preceding All Saints Day or All Hallows Day on the 1st of November. Over time, All Hallows Eve became Halloween. Some believe it replaced an earlier pagan Celtic festival called *Samhain* (Scottish Gaelic for summer's end) that marked the onset of winter and was associated, in Ireland, with the supernatural.

Trick or Treat!

This involves visiting neighbours in costume on the promise of free sugary snacks. The tradition is thought to originate in Samhain practices, where people wore animal skins to ward off unwanted spirits. Other common observances include gothic décor, pumpkin carving and watching horror films.

A Carved Halloween Pumpkin

Halloween Costumes

HISTORIC HAUNTINGS

Besides ancient myths and legends, people have also recorded personal encounters with ghosts. While the oldest surviving report of a haunting came from ancient Greece, it is likely many experiences have been lost or passed into legend through oral tradition.

Athenian Apparition
Athens, Greece, 1st Century BCE

The oldest recorded haunting comes from a letter dated around 100 CE. The ancient Roman author Pliny the Younger penned the letter to a friend, describing an old haunting with some glee. According to the letter, tenants fled a house in Athens due to strange noises and the apparition of a ghost. Luckily the stoic philosopher Athenodorus Cananites took over the house and appeased the ghost by giving its long-forgotten corpse a proper burial.

Drummer Of Tedworth
Tedworth, England, Circa 1661-1663

In 1661, landowner John Mompesson experienced one of the first reported poltergeist hauntings in England. The event was characterised by phantom drumming sounds and the movement of objects around his home. The haunting drew visitors from all around the country, including Christopher Wren (architect of St. Paul's Cathedral) and clergyman Joseph Glanvill.

Claw-like marks were discovered in soot.

The Ghost Hunter

Glanvill undertook a thorough investigation of the property, making him a progenitor ghost hunter. His posthumously released book *Saducismus Triumphatus* (1683) recounts his Tedworth experience amongst other evidence for magic, ghosts and witchcraft. Later sceptics suggested Mompesson's daughter was responsible for hoaxing the activity. Whether this accusation is fair or not, the blaming of children for paranormal activity is common in sceptic literature.

Despite all the activity, no one actually saw a ghost.

Joseph Glanvill

DEMONS

In myth and legend, demons are inhuman spirits often associated with mischief or evil. Despite being distinct from traditional ghosts, demon hauntings can be very similar. For example, they are believed to move objects, make strange sounds and be a nuisance.

Ancient Gods

Christian mythologies exhibit a colourful gallery of demons, each believed to be a fallen angel. Many of their names refer to beliefs that predate the Bible, such as *Moloch* (a bull headed deity or form of sacrifice).

Tricksters

Jinn encompass a broad variety of paranormal forces, most often associated with trickster and wish-granting spirits. A famous lamp-dwelling Jinn or Genie appears in the ancient tale Aladdin.

Demon Disguise

In the 16th century, much of the Protestant establishment rejected Catholic beliefs in limbo and ghosts. Instead, they taught that the devil and his demons were responsible for hauntings. Despite this attitude, entrenched folk belief in ghosts continued.

Japanese theatrical demon mask

Mesopotamian demon statuette

Thai Yaksha temple guardian

SPIRITUAL COMMUNICATION

For thousands of years, people have tried to summon ghosts through ritual magic. Practitioners distinguish two types of summoning called invocation and evocation. Invocation invites a spirit to possess someone, while evocation encourages a spirit to appear in a convenient place, such as a parlour or secret dungeon.

Summoners believe ghosts can help heal sickness, impart knowledge or even attack enemies.

Noaidi
To the Sami peoples of Nordic Europe, those who talked to the spirit world were called *noaidi*. Noaidi asked the spirits for favourable hunting hauls and weather.

Jhākri
In Nepal, practitioners are called *Jhākri*. Traditionally they brandish a drum called a *dhyāngro*, which is used during rituals. Besides blessings and magical cures, they are employed to invoke ancestral ghosts.

Mu
In Korean cultures, those who commune with spirits are often called *Mu*. Their rituals typically involve bright costumes and dancing.

Plastic Shaman
Traditional practices are sometimes wrongfully appropriated by people from outside of the respective culture. Native American campaigners call these cultural frauds *plastic shamans*.

FREAKY FORTIFICATIONS

Castles are commonly identified as the sites of ghost legends. Their battles, deadly dungeons and historical figures make them perfect vessels for storytelling.

Himeji Castle
Himeji, Japan, Circa 14th Century

The 14th century Himeji Castle in southern Japan is believed to host several ghosts within its gleaming white walls. In one legend, the servant Okiku was murdered after refusing the advances of her samurai master. The samurai falsely accused her of stealing a precious plate and threw her in the well. Soon, her ghost could be heard counting plates, forever dismayed by the missing crockery. In some tellings, her ghost crawled from the well to torment her killer. The tale may have inspired aspects of the horror novel *Ring* (1991) and the subsequent film adaptations.

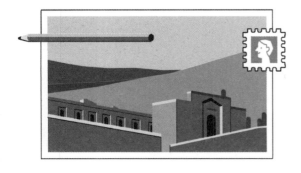

Bhangarh Fort
Rajasthan, India, Circa 16th Century

Legend suggests this castle is haunted
after being cursed by an angry wizard.

Zvíkov Castle
Zvíkovské Podhradí, Czechia, Circa 13th Century

Haunted by a ghost that preys
on electronics and animals.

Edinburgh Castle
Edinburgh, Scotland, UK, Circa 12th Century

Often attributed the title of the UK's
'most haunted' castle in tourism materials.

Predjama Castle
Predjama, Slovenia, Circa 13th Century

One legend pertains to the Knight Erasmus,
who reputedly haunts the castle after
he was murdered on the toilet.

Houska Castle
Blatce, Czechia, Circa 13th Century

Legends assert the castle is built
around a gate to hell.

Kinnitty Castle
Kinnitty, Ireland, Circa 19th Century

The latest castle to sit on a plot occupied
for over a millennium. Believed to be
haunted by all manner of ghosts.

SPIRITUAL PROTECTION

Belief in ghosts and evil spirits have prompted many cultures to develop protective measures. Practices come in many shapes and sizes, from amulets to magic rituals. The practice of averting evil is called apotropaic magic (from the Greek for ward off).

Ifrit

In ancient Egypt and neighbouring Middle Eastern regions some believed the scenes of murders were haunted by vengeful spirits called *Ifrit*. In some practices, nails were driven into the murder location to appease the spirit.

Lemures

The ancient Romans called vengeful ghosts *Lemures*. During the festival of Lemuria, Romans banished Lemures by hosting loud parties, and ritualistically throwing beans.

Gorgoneion

Ancient Greek architecture often features imagery associated with the gorgons (monsters in Greek mythology) to frighten away evil spirits. They are often represented in carvings, reliefs and mosaics.

Spiderweb Charm

The Ojibwe people in North America have an ancient tradition of making spiderweb-like charms to capture evil spirits and nightmares. Today, the charm is most often called a dreamcatcher.

Grotesqueries

From the Middle Ages, European churches and castles featured monstrous stone carvings. These leering faces were thought to prevent the entry of evil spirits and the devil. Grotesqueries are also used on roofs to redirect rainwater and are called gargoyles.

Horseshoes

An ancient practice with origins in the Middle East saw iron horseshoes mounted above doorways to ward off evil spirits. In Europe, the practice became associated with Christianity due to a 10th century legend in which the English Bishop Dunstan thwarted the devil with a horseshoe.

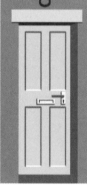

Evil Eye

One of the most common practices of apotropaic magic is the use of amulets to protect against the Evil Eye. Originating in ancient Mediterranean and Middle East cultures, the Evil Eye is believed to be a sort of directed curse. In many cases Evil Eye amulets are also used to protect against ghosts and inhuman spirits.

COCK LANE GHOST

Cock Lane
London, UK, 1762

One of the most famous hauntings in the UK took place in an 18th Century London house. Following the death of Fanny Lynes, her ghost (dubbed Scratching Fanny) was reputed to communicate by knocking and scratching around her former lodgings.

The boasts of landlord Richard Parsons encouraged vast crowds of sightseers to visit. Prolific figures included the politician Horace Walpole and the Prince of York. At the time, Methodists were associated with belief in the paranormal. This led suspicious Anglican figures to accuse Methodist clergymen of drumming up hysteria.

Street chaos and scandalous reportage prompted a committee of intellectuals to investigate. Samuel Johnson (creator of the dictionary) attended and decided that Parsons' daughter had performed a hoax. This was later affirmed by the discovery of a piece of wood on her person that were used to make the scratching noises and knockings of the ghost. A later trial found Richard Parsons guilty of defaming Lynes's widower and was sentenced to two years in prison.

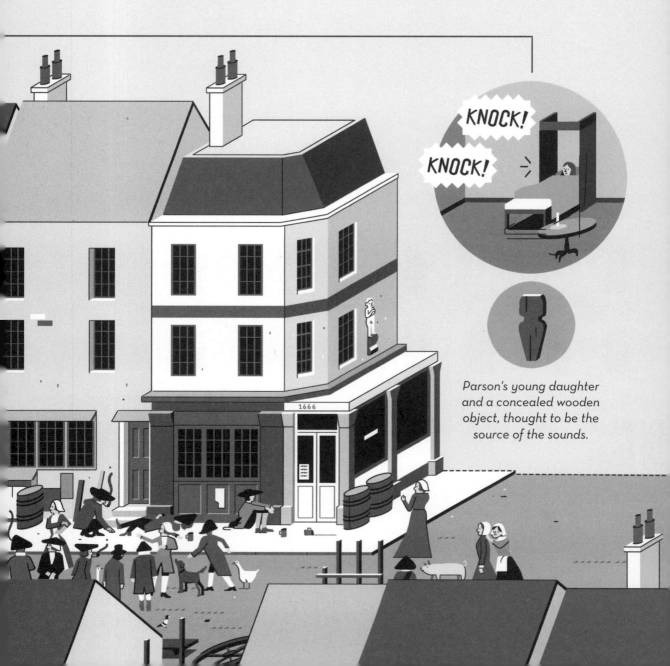

Parson's young daughter and a concealed wooden object, thought to be the source of the sounds.

THE 19th CENTURY

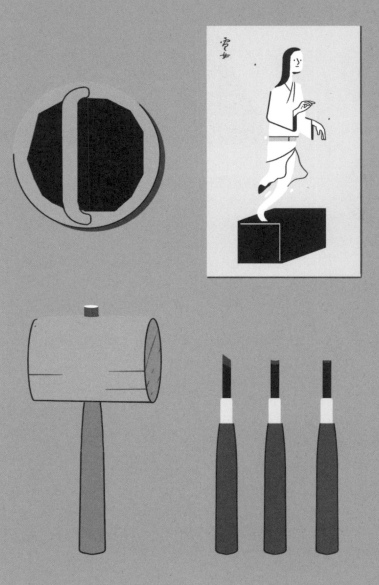

Yūrei woodblock print (circa 1850)

SPIRITUALISM

Following the traumatic American Civil War, a bereaved public sought radical new ideas. Alongside reformists, socialists and women's rights activists, a religious movement known as Spiritualism rose to prominence.

Maggie Fox

Kate Fox

Leah Fox

The Fox Sisters
Hydesville, NY, USA, 1848

Spiritualism was primarily concerned with trying to contact ghosts through ritual *séances* (from the French word for session). Séances were popularised by the Fox Sisters from Hydesville, New York. From 1848, Maggie and Kate Fox performed around the country as spirit mediums (from the Latin *medius* for middle), during which they interpreted apparently phantom knockings as ghostly messages.

Harassment

Male sceptics tried to expose the Fox's as frauds by wrongly and intrusively probing their bodies and clothing. In fact, the Fox sisters were underage teens, who alongside other mediums, were often exploited and harassed by debunkers to undress. Men of science who abused their privileges might be better considered men of fraud.

The stress of touring and scrutiny led to alcohol addiction and the fracturing of the Fox's sisterly bond. In 1888 a reporter offered Maggie $1,500 to confess their deception, and she soon detailed how the knocking sounds were achieved by the cracking of joints in their feet.

A New Religion

Spiritualism proved to be a profitable enterprise for mediums and delivered a catharsis for the bereaved. The movement was characteristically popular amongst the white middle classes of America and was soon exported to Europe.

Influential Spiritualists

Arthur Conan Doyle, Writer

Victoria Woodhull, Politician

W.B. Yeats, Poet

William Frank Taylor, Priest

THE BIRTHPLACE OF
MODERN SPIRITUALISM
UPON THIS SITE STOOD THE HYDESVILLE COTTAGE
THE HOME OF THE
FOX SISTERS
THROUGH WHICH MEDIUMSHIP COMMUNICATION
WITH THE SPIRIT WORLD WAS ESTABLISHED
MARCH 31, 1848
THERE IS NO DEATH
THERE ARE NO DEAD
PLACED HERE BY M E CADWALLADER
DEC 1927

Birthplace of Spiritualism

A monument and small museum mark the spot where the Fox sisters once lived in Rochester. An inscription reads: 'There is no death, there are no dead'.

Theosophy

In the 1870s, the Ukrainian occultist Helena Blavatsky developed a spin-off religious movement called Theosophy. In Theosophy, séances were conducted with spirits called Ascended Masters. Unlike regular ghosts of the dead, it was believed these masters were mortals who had separated body and soul through enlightenment.

MEDIUMSHIP

During the heights of Spiritualism, mediums were a popular booking for private events and public theatres. Performances were made in the dark as mediums claimed that ghosts abhorred light. Sceptics suggested the only purpose of dim lighting was to conceal fakery.

Wonder Women

Many mediums were women, and they enjoyed the freedom to travel, earn their own money and move between social strata. Unfortunately, like the Fox sisters, many were wrongly restrained and harassed. The medium Emma Hardinge Britten took legal action against fans who stalked her and sent love letters.

Séance
In the most popular form of séances, participants sat around a table with hands touching in a dark room. Mediums led sessions and conveyed apparent messages from ghosts.

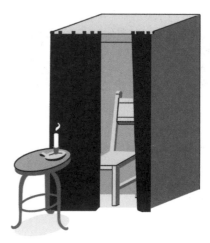

Spirit Cabinet
Some mediums conducted their séances from a small booth or cabinet.

Thrilling Theatrics
Many mediums wore theatrical costumes or involved unique gimmicks to make their performances more exciting.

Ectoplasm
A white goo ejected from the mouth. Many believed ectoplasm to be spiritual energy. Hoaxers were often caught using cloth to produce the effect. The term was coined by French doctor Charles Richet, using the Greek for outside plasma.

Forward Thinking

Mediums were often friendly with progressive freethinkers who championed women's liberation and social reform. Many mediums used the veil of their mediumship to broadcast political messages. Some mediums, men and women, engaged in consensual erotic acts, such as being tied up or performing in their underwear. The English medium Annie Fairlamb Mellon kissed women and men under the guise of spiritual invocation.

The Davenport Brothers' Spirit Cabinet
During performances the brothers were tied up inside a cabinet filled with instruments. Once the doors closed the instruments would sound as if activated by ghosts.

Houdini's Margery Box
A box built to test the authenticity of mediums by limiting their movement.

Spirit Writing
Some mediums conveyed apparent spirit messages on paper. Typical performances were involved blindfolds to reduce obvious suspicion of fraud.

YŪREI

Eerie Art

In Japanese mythology, ghosts are called *Yūrei* (meaning faint or dim spirit). In the 19th century, Yūrei were popular subjects in theatre and on woodblock prints. There are many types of Yūrei, each said to haunt the earth for different grievances endured in life.

1. **Onryō**
    Ghosts that lust for revenge against those who wronged them.

2. **Funayūrei**
    A subset of vengeful *Onryō* that died at sea. They are sometimes fish-like in appearance.

3. **Fuyūrei**
    Floating, aimless spirits.

4. **Goryō**
    Vengeful aristocrats, capable of summoning natural disasters.

5. **Jibakurei**
Similar to the aimless *Fuyūrei*, except bound to a particular location.

6. **Zashiki-warashi**
The mischievous ghosts of children.

7. **Ubume**
The ghost of a mother who died in childbirth. They are said to provide gifts to any surviving children.

8. **Woeful Women**
In art, Yūrei are commonly depicted as white-clad women with sickly expressions and tangled hair, not far removed from depictions of ghosts in modern cinema. Modern writers suggest the femininity of ghosts in many cultures is representative of common stereotypes – that 'emotional' women are more likely to linger as ghosts after death.

NORTH AMERICAN GHOST LEGENDS

North America is home to a vast number of ghost legends and many can be traced to the mythologies of Native Americans, while others are influenced by the heritage of settlers from the Old World.

The Bell Witch
Bell Ranch, TN, USA, Circa 1817–1821

According to legend, Bell Ranch was besieged by a talkative ghost, who locals identified as Kate Batts, a local witch. The ghost took great pleasure in berating the ranchers with insults and stunning supernatural powers. For reasons best known to itself, it apparently turned a man into a mule, aported objects and injured ranch inhabitants. The head rancher John Bell allegedly died in his bed, following weeks of spectral taunting and ailments.

Bell Ranch

Monstrous apparitions

John Bell's attempt to throw the witch ghost into the fireplace

Great Dismal Swamp
Virginia and North Carolina, USA,
Circa 18ᵗʰ Century

These sprawling alligator-filled marshes were inhabited for over 13,000 years by coastal communities of Native Americans. European explorers in the 18ᵗʰ century offered a negative appraisal and named it the Great Dismal Swamp and French speakers called it the *Marais Maudit*, or cursed swamp.

With thick fog, damp earth and the groans of amphibians, birds and reptiles, it is easy to understand why the swamp might have attracted a good number of ghost legends.

The ghost named *The Lady of the Lake* is said to paddle her canoe through the mists, lit only by fireflies. Besides the lone paddler, phantom figures, ships and lights reputedly stalk the green waters.

TALKING BOARDS

Planchette

In the 1850s, European product designers commodified mediumship by selling a pencil-wielding wooden pallet on wheels called a *planchette* (French for little plank). It was believed that participants could place their hands on the planchette, and spirits would guide their hands to make it draw shapes and letters.

GW Cottrell (1859)

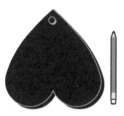

Kirkby & Co (1869)

Ouija Board (1890)

Espirito Talking Board (1891)

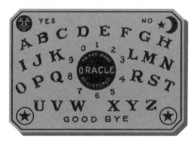

Mystifying Oracle (1915)

Mystiscope Fortune Teller (1925)

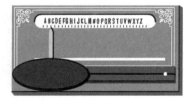

Telepathic Spirit Communicator (1936)

Hasko Mystic Board (1940)

Mystic Answer Board (1944)

Spirit Boards

A more popular design called a spirit board utilised a miniature planchette which, when held correctly, would seemingly point to letters and numbers rendered on a large board. The most famous example called *Ouija* was developed by American inventor Elijah Bond. A multitude of imitators soon followed, and copyright battles raged. Sceptics believe that planchette and similar devices are not guided by ghosts, but rather the ideomotor effect (the involuntary twitching of participants).

Ouija Board – Deluxe Edition (1967)   Transogram (1967)

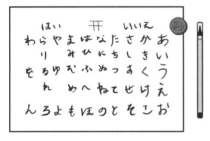

Kokkuri-San (1970s)   Ouija for Windows (1993)

Charmed Spirit Board (2006)   Ouija Board (2008)   Talking Board (2015)

INFAMOUS ISOLATION

Phare De Tévennec
The coast of France, 19th Century

Besides places with strong historical connections, remote structures often seem to accumulate ghost legends. Built in 1875, the French lighthouse *Phare De Tévennec* has attracted a respectable amount of ghost stories. In its early years, the lighthouse was manned by solitary lightkeepers. According to legend, the first caretaker Henri Guezennec was driven to madness by the voices of dead sailors that plagued the area. The newspaper *Le Télégramme* reported that crucifixes were affixed to the rocks surrounding the lighthouse in an attempt to exorcise the troublesome spirits. Time and tide, however, has seen to their removal.

SPIRIT PHOTOGRAPHY

In the 19th century it became popular for photographers to sell 'real' ghost pictures made in a studio or at a séance.

Stereoscopic Spectres

The London Stereoscopic Company specialised in selling photos with a 3D effect. In the 1850s they sold implicitly staged pictures featuring ghosts.

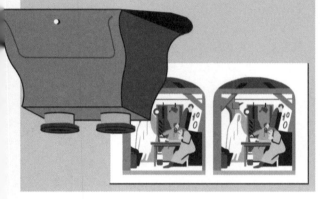

Deathly Dolls

In the 1870s, French medium Édouard Isidore Buguet created miniature dolls to model as ghosts in his double-exposed photographs. Buguet was unable to evade the justice system and was jailed for fraud.

Double Exposure

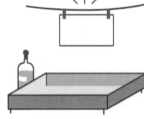

Used photo plate inserted in camera

Portrait taken

Photograph developed with overlapping images

Mysterious 'ghost' appears on photo

Mumler's Memorabilia

William Mumler discovered, in the 1860s, that mixing photographic negatives could create ghost-like figures. Mumler's wife Hannah happened to be a business-savvy medium. Together, they sold photographs starring the late family members of clients. After the American Civil War, there was large market of bereaved clients. One famous client was Mary Todd Lincoln, the widow of the late president. During a trial, Mumler was accused and acquitted of fraud, but his reputation was forever damaged.

CLUBS AND SOCIETIES

Following the excitement of 19th century Spiritualism in the West, groups of intellectuals and enthusiasts formed groups to study and discuss ghost phenomena. The study of strange phenomena has often been retitled according to fashion. Common vernacular includes; psychical research, parapsychology, supernatural and paranormal.

William Crookes *Charles Dickens*

The Ghost Club
The Ghost Club was founded in 1862 in London. Its members were joined by many influential people such as writers Charles Dickens and W.B. Yeats, and scientist William Crookes. The club still operates today and is the longest known running ghost club.

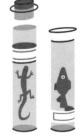

Medium outfit. *Collection of reputedly apported objects.*

Society of Psychical Research (SPR)
Founded in 1882, the SPR gathered data on telepathy (a term coined by member Frederic Myers), hypnotism and séances. Though they worked to expose fakes, the SPR also collaborated with mediums they believed genuine. The SPR remains in operation today with field investigation, analysis and publications.

Metaphysical Laboratory
Hungarian chemist Elemér Chengery Pap performed numerous experiments from 1928. The lab particularly focused on the medium trick of apporting objects from thin air. He dressed mediums in futuristic overalls in an attempt to eliminate conjurer's tricks.

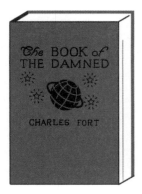

Fortean Society

American writer Charles Hoy Fort's *Book of the Damned* (1919) is thought to be the first comprehensive collection of odd phenomena. In 1931, fans began the Fortean Society in New York City to discuss esoteric subjects. They shared a newsletter called *Doubt*, which was succeeded by the more official and influential magazine *The Fortean Times*.

Australian Institute of Parapsychological Research (AIPR)

Founded in 1977, the AIPR studies a broad range of paranormal phenomena. As an organisation, one of their aims is to place phenomena in the context of experience, health and illness.

French researcher Eugène Osty invented an infrared camera trigger to monitor mediums in the dark.

Institut Métapsychique International (IMI)

The French IMI was founded in 1919 to study a range of phenomena. Lead researchers such as Dr. Gustave Geley directed efforts towards scrutinising mediums. Today the IMI continues to assist and train academics and students interested in the paranormal.

ESP Studies

The US military's Stargate Project attempted to find practical applications for psychic abilities in the 1970s. They believed 'remote viewing' could be used to learn enemy secrets. Their efforts were famously covered in Jon Ronson's book *The Men Who Stare at Goats* (2004).

ARCHITECTURAL AUTEUR

Winchester Mystery House
San Jose, CA, USA

In 1884, Sarah Winchester, wife and heiress of the late gun magnate began converting a San Jose farmhouse into a sprawling labyrinth. Winchester had an uncompromising creative vision and drew up the architectural plans herself, with influences from occult symbolism. Winchester playfully renovated the house's layout following earthquake damage in 1906. The resulting structure's oddly placed doors, stairs and uneven floors have a disconcerting effect.

Sarah Winchester

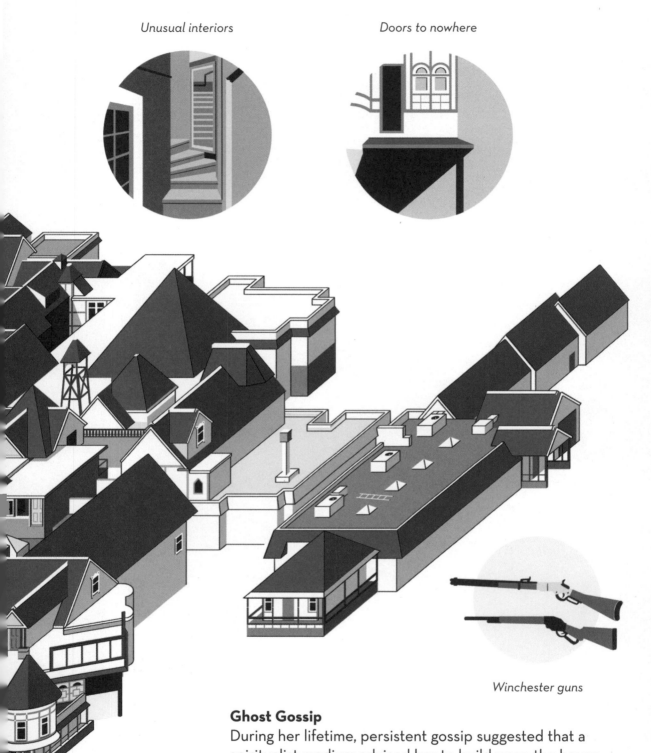

Unusual interiors

Doors to nowhere

Winchester guns

Ghost Gossip

During her lifetime, persistent gossip suggested that a spiritualist medium advised her to build upon the house continuously. The Herculean labour would apparently appease the ghosts of people who were killed by Winchester guns. Gossip became legend, which today is touted by tour guides, ghost hunters and a gift shop.

THE 20th CENTURY

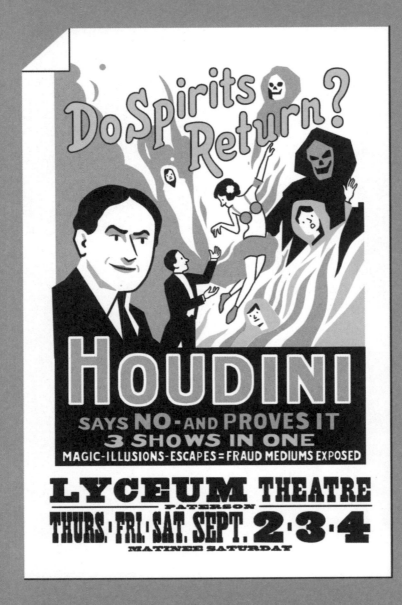

Houdini promotional poster (1909)

DEBUNKERY

In the 20th century, sceptics continued to debunk ghost belief, which many believed to be symptomatic of superstition and medium deception. American magician Harry Houdini was appalled to see some mediums use stage magic to perform routines he considered exploitive. Rose 'Mac' Mackenberg was the chief investigator for Houdini's campaign. To gather evidence, Mac worked undercover whilst wearing imaginative disguises.

A spirit trumpet.

Mac's many disguises.

Magic Tricks

Common fakery was exposed in pamphlets, books and during stage performances, such as those by Houdini. Tricks were engineered by mediums and their stooges (assistants). Children made good stooges as their stature made them less detectable in the dark.

HULLO...

Spirit trumpets were typically used to amplify the voice of a spirit that had allegedly inhabited a medium.

Special hooks attached to mediums' clothing could move tables without need of their hands.

Information could be conveyed
to mediums through hidden
Morse Code devices.

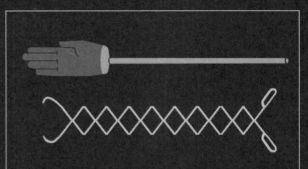

Glowing objects hung from a string
were used to make ghostly lights.

POKE!

Extending arms were used
to poke sitters remotely.

Under the cover of darkness, levitation
could be faked with various props.

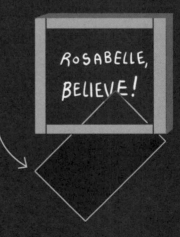

ROSABELLE,
BELIEVE!

Special pads were engineered
to reveal spirit writing.

THOUGHTFORMS

In occult theory, a thoughtform is the transfer of an idea through psychic powers. Members of the Theosophical Society, Annie Besant and C.W. Leadbeater described the phenomena in their book *Thought Forms* (1909) as radiant vibrations and floating lights. Some proponents believed that ghosts were created by unfocused thoughtforms.

Thoughtforms, as depicted in 20ᵗʰ century art.

Artistic Abstraction

Thought Forms contained vibrant and imaginative paintings of its subject matter. Their deviations from unfashionable 19ᵗʰ century literalism influenced many burgeoning abstract artists. Painters such as Wassily Kandinsky, Kazimir Malevich and Piet Mondrian all took inspiration from spiritualist and theosophist theories.

Tulpa

Thoughtforms are similar to the Tibetan concept of a *tulpa*. Tulpas are objects or beings thought to be created through mental or spiritual powers. They supposedly take on a life of their own as a person or creature. Ghost hunter Ed Warren speculated that cryptids (mysterious creatures) such as Bigfoot were actually tulpas manifested by psychics.

HAUNTED RUINS

Skeletal ruins of houses stand as mysterious monuments to their previous occupants. The more tragic circumstances of ruin foster legends of haunting. During the 20th century, automobiles and air travel enabled informal tourism centred around reputedly haunted sites.

Kinarut Mansion, Malaysia, abandoned circa 1920s

An abandoned manor house found in a forested area of eastern Malaysia. Today, the mansion is maintained as a historic attraction and legends have spread that it is home to a plethora of spirits.

Lui Family Mansion, abandoned circa 1950s

Known colloquially as the *Minxiong Ghost House*, this grand baroque-style property has been completely encased by foliage. The property is reputedly haunted by the ghost of a maid who drowned in the property's well.

La Casa Embrujada, abandoned in 2013

Directly translated, *The Haunted House* entered local legend in 2013 after a reputed cultist died by suicide on the property. To discourage ghost hunting trespassers a large sign bears the disclaimer 'This is Not a Haunted House'.

GHOST HUNTERS

Ghost hunting is the practice of investigating alleged hauntings to look for proof of ghosts or a rational, scientific explanation. While there is no singular pedagogy, ghost hunting typically involves the structured investigations of reportedly haunted places. During the 20th century, the most famous ghost hunters were typically white middle-class men from the USA and UK.

1. Interview
A witness or property owner is interviewed by the investigators.

2. Planning and Research
The locale of a haunting is surveyed in daylight to familiarise the layout. Additional background information about the location is uncovered in libraries and online.

3. Site Investigation
Ghost hunting is typically a night-time activity dating back to the era of mediumship. Today, some shirk tradition and insist on daylight observation.

4. Vigil
Ghost hunters remain in the locale until the early hours.

5. Debrief
Data collected from the site is studied and discussed.

6. Hypothesis
The investigators try to explain paranormal experiences.

7. Feedback
Investigators report back to the client and make suggestions. For example, if carbon monoxide is discovered they will defer to a gas engineer to resolve the problem.

TOOLS OF THE TRADE

Paranormal investigators use a range of tools to discover reputed evidence of the ghosts, or rational explanations for hauntings.

Pen and Paper
An investigator records witness statements, weather conditions and draws intricate floor plans.

Flour
Flour, chalk and other powders have been used to reveal footprints of hoaxers.

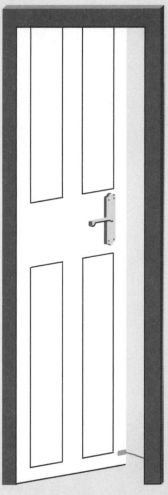

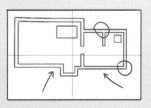

Map and Survey
Surveying a property can reveal blind spots, strange shadows and other architectural oddities that may cause bizarre experiences.

Cameras
Used in attempt to capture a picture of a ghost.

Trip Wires
Thread has been used to catch frauds sneaking through hallways and doors.

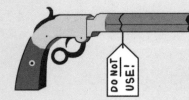

Armaments
Some historic ghost hunters carried guns. As of yet, no one has successfully maimed a ghost.

Laser Thermometers
Some use laser thermometers detect 'cold spots' made by ghosts. These devices only measure surface temperature, and are not always accurate.

Sound Recorders
Used in attempt to capture the voices of ghosts, known as electronic voice phenomena (EVP).

Dogs
Ghost hunters have been known to bring along faithful companions to detect ghosts. Critics of the practice suggest leading a dog around in a dark building filled with anxious ghost hunters is a silly idea.

Carbon Monoxide Detector
Carbon monoxide poisoning can cause a range of symptoms associated with hauntings and is very dangerous. Detecting its presence can help prevent illness and death.

Electromagnetic Field Meter (EMF)
Some believe they can detect ghosts in the fluctuations of EMF. EMF meters are actually designed to monitor wiring and appliances.

Air Ion Counter
Atmospheres with high ion counts may cause a range of mild symptoms associated with hauntings, such as unusual fatigue.

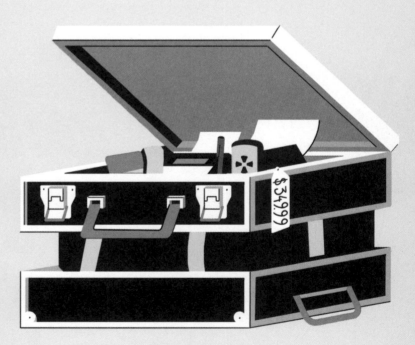

Infrared (IR) Camera
Invisible to the human eye, IR radiation is emitted by all objects. IR cameras are deployed as night vision by teams to record goings on in the dark.

Commercial Ghost Hunting Kits
Pre-packaged sets of equipment for eye-watering prices.

WAR GHOSTS

Battlefields are often considered to be haunted due to their scenes of suffering, death and disease. During the 20th century, this ghostly association was encouraged in patriotic fables and psychological warfare.

The Angels of Mons

In 1914, Welsh author Arthur Machen wrote a newspaper story about ghosts on the battlefield. In the story, ghost bowmen from the historic Battle of Agincourt helped British troops survive a battle with German forces. Following publication, a surprised Machen discovered readers believed his yarn. English journalist David Clarke suggests the story was encouraged by British authorities as war propaganda.

Wandering Souls

During the Vietnam War, US military engineers attempted to undermine the morale of the Viet Cong by playing ghostly voices through speaker installations. The US military hoped to exploit what they understood of the local belief systems – that the Vietnamese believed ghosts were caused by the improperly buried dead. It is unknown how successful the audio campaign really was as it usually only prompted the Viet Cong to open fire on the speakers.

WOOAAAAH!'s

Ghost soldiers are commonly featured in legends around the world

Knights
Europe

Roman Centurions
Europe

Civil War Soldiers
USA

WW1 Soldiers
Worldwide

WW2 Soldiers
Worldwide

MOST HAUNTED

Borley Rectory
Borley, Essex, United Kingdom, 1927–1938

Described as the 'Most Haunted House in Britain' by ghost hunter Harry Price, Borley Rectory was home to many ghostly disturbances and investigations over several decades. As there is no empirical method to detect degrees of haunting, the title 'most haunted' was attributed based on reputation.

Skull

Harry Price, ghost hunter

Ghostly writing

'Ghost nun' reputedly seen at property

In 1927, Reverend Guy Eric Smith and wife Mabel moved into the Borley Rectory, finding it to be draughty and old fashioned. To make matters worse, the couple found a human skull and saw a ghost in the garden.

Harry Price briefly investigated in 1929 and recorded all sorts of paranormal activity, including the throwing of objects. After his reports to newspapers, the rectory became a popular destination for paranormal tourists.

'Trigger objects' were placed around the house to encourage poltergeist activity.

A map of Borley Rectory

In 1937, Price recruited 48 volunteers to observe the property, on the condition they follow a set of rules. Caretakers took notes, drew maps and entertained themselves with planchette but were unable to find any conclusive evidence of haunting.

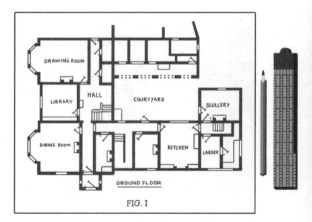

LIMINAL SPACE

Some locations owe much of their haunted reputation to their frightful aspect. Tunnels are thresholds between light and dark, making them liminal spaces. Many tunnels around the world are thought to be haunted and carry burdensome legends of ghosts.

Kiyotaki Tunne
Kyoto, Japan, 1929

The Kiyotaki Tunnel in Japan is popular amongst paranormal tourists. However, terse signs warn visitors against the dangers of walking into an active tunnel. Built in 1929, the narrow tunnel is flanked by dark woods and traffic lights. Ghost legends often feature a conditional quality, such as a preferable time, weather condition or date best suited for the sighting of a ghost. In this case, the nearby traffic light is said to suddenly light green when a ghost is present. Following an earthquake in 1968, repair workers discovered aged bones and a shattered skull amongst the deluge of rubble, presumably belonging to a those who died during the original construction.

SIMULATED HAUNTINGS

In lieu of reliable and marketable hauntings, 20th century engineers built simulated attractions. The most popular attractions, the *Haunted House* and *Ghost Train* may still be found in theme parks and fun fairs to this day.

Ghost Train

The first ghost train ride opened in 1930 on the Blackpool Pleasure Beach in England. Imported from America as a Pretzel Ride (so named due to the knotted corridors within), the ride was renamed in reference to the popular play *The Ghost Train* (1923).

Actors and crew at simulated attractions

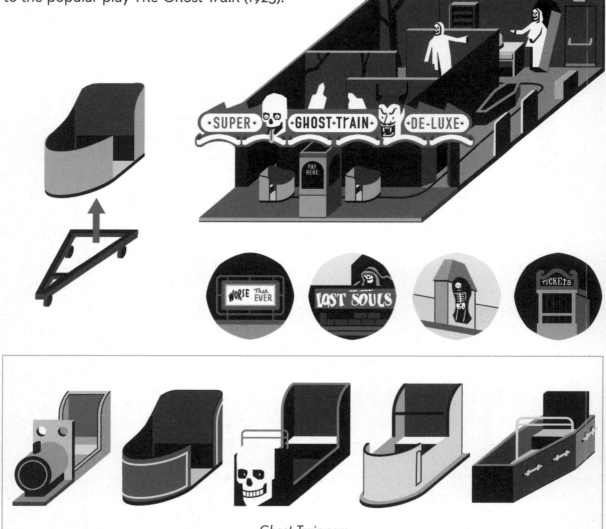

Ghost Train cars

Haunted Houses

The simulated haunted house involves customers wandering around a structure filled with frightful decor and actors. Simulated haunted houses rose to prominence in 1920s America and were often staged by magicians. Since then, they have become more sophisticated and convincing with the aid of animatronics, optical illusions, and set-dressing comparable to a Hollywood film production.

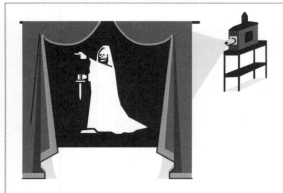

Phantasmagoria

Phantasmagorias were theatrical stagings of the supernatural, aided by magic lanterns (lamp-lit projectors), sets and actors. Likely first established in 17th century Germany, phantasmagorias were used to delight audiences and aid in fraudulent séances.

TIMESLIPS

Some individuals have reported coming across people and places from another time period. British poet and psychical researcher Frederic W. H. Myers called this retrocognition. It is more commonly known as timeslips, where experiences are characterised by ghost-like figures and visions.

Palace of Versailles, France
In 1901, English academics Charlotte Anne Moberly and Eleanor Jourdain apparently wandered into an 18th century version of the Palace of Versailles. One sceptic theory asserts the pair crashed an avant-garde LGBTQ+ party, as poet Robert de Montesquiou hosted fancy dress parties in the area.

Bold Street, Liverpool, UK
There are several accounts of reputed time travel in the vicinity of Bold Street. In one case a police officer briefly found himself surrounded by 1950s fashion and shops. In a newspaper report one man described his surprise to find himself specifically in 1967.

Mokele-Mbembe, Congo River Basin
Mokele-Mbembe is a reputed sauropod dinosaur sighted in Central Africa. Some believe the sauropod has miraculously survived extinction. Others believe the creature stumbled upon its own dramatic timeslip.

DOPPELGÄNGERS

Doppelgängers (German for double-goer) are ghostly doubles of living people. Their reputed behaviours range from the sinister to the mundane. In her influential ghost compendium *Night Side of Nature* (1848), Catherine Crowe observed doppelgängers were most sighted when people were ill or asleep. Psychologists attribute the phenomena to a hallucination called autoscopy (from the Greek for self watcher).

THE MIDCENTURY

The Innocents film poster (1961)

PHANTOM VEHICLES

As cars became increasingly ubiquitous in the 20th century, some suspicious minds considered their quirks as evidence of haunting. Common in urban legends, phantom vehicles are reported to haunt land, air and sea. Some believe they are haunted by their former owners or bare a dreadful curse.

1. **The Number 7 Bus (London, UK, 1934)**
   A ghostly bus that ran drivers off the road.

2. **Vauxhall Astra (A3, Surrey, UK, 2003)**
   The sighting of a phantom car led police to find a wreck and dead driver that had gone unnoticed for five months.

3. **Yellow Beetle (Kuala Lumpur, Malaysia 1990s)**
   A VW Beetle believed to haunt roads.

4. **The Flying Dutchman (Atlantic Ocean, 16th Century)**
   A large ship crewed by ghosts.

5. **Silverpilen (Stockholm, Sweden, 1980s)**
   Swedish for Silver Arrow, the SIlverpilen is a ghost train believed to haunt the Stockholm Metro.

6. **Flight 401 (Florida, USA, 1971)**
   Following a crash in which over one hundred people died, parts of the Eastern Air Lines plane were salvaged and used in other craft. Rumours soon spread that planes equipped with parts from plane flight 401 were haunted.

7. **USS Zaca (Monaco, 1959)**
   A yacht once owned by Australian actor Errol Flynn. Following his death, the yacht was thought to be haunted and received the attention of Catholic exorcists in 1979.

8. **Death Coach (Europe, 18th Century)**
   A legendary ghost-driven carriage.

9. **Phantom Phaeton (Present, Military History Museum, Vienna, Austria)**
   The car in which Archduke Franz Ferdinand of Austria was assassinated. Legends of the car being haunted first circulated in the 1950s.

10. **SM-UB-65 (Atlantic Ocean, 1918)**
    According to legend this German submarine was plagued with crew deaths and ghosts.

FREAKY FIGURINES

Isla De Las Muñecas
Xochimilco, Mexico, Circa 1950s

In the canals of Xochimilco, a small island bears hundreds
of artfully arranged dolls. According to legend, the island's
owner, Don Julián Santana Barrera installed the dolls
to appease the ghost of a drowned girl.

The crew from the TV show *Ghost Adventures*,
who visited the island in 2014 and were delighted by
the general atmosphere and strange sounds they heard.

La Recoleta Cemetery
Buenos Aires, Argentina, Circa 19th Century to Present

Built in 1822, this Argentinian cemetery boasts a fantastic labyrinth of mausoleums. Much like any other burial site, it has attracted a great many ghost stories. According to legend, the teenager Rufina Cambacérès was entombed alive after a comatose state was mistaken for death. Her ghost is said to wander the graves, calling for help. In the 19th century, some people bought emergency bells that could be operated from within the grave, this is where the idiom 'saved by the bell' originates.

Distinctively ornate tombs contribute to the haunted reputation.

Grave Diggers' Ghost
Known for a disembodied sound of keys jangling.

La Dama de Blanco
A legendary white lady, adapted into the film Fantasmas de Buenos Aires (1942).

Rufina Cambacérès
Reputedly seen lurking around her own tomb.

ANOTHER LAND

Some believe ghosts are from other dimensions. This hypothesis was especially popular with UFO enthusiasts and is a common feature in science fiction.

Passport to Magonia
In his book *Passport to Magonia* (1969) astronomer and UFO enthusiast Jacques Vallée drew comparisons between 20th century alien UFO encounters and the historic tales of elemental spirits from mystic lands such as færie. Vallée suggested all paranormal events were conducted by an extra-dimensional force.

Into the Goblin Universe
English journalist Ted Holiday's posthumously released book *The Goblin Universe* (1990) blamed a higher intelligence for everything from the Loch Ness Monster to poltergeists and UFOs. The text also takes a worrying swerve to critique the theory of evolution.

From Etheria, with Love
During the 1950s, American parapsychologist Meade Layne proposed that UFOs originated from a dimension he dubbed *Etheria*. Layne's speculations were based on conversations with spiritual medium Mark Probert, to whom Etherians made apparent contact.

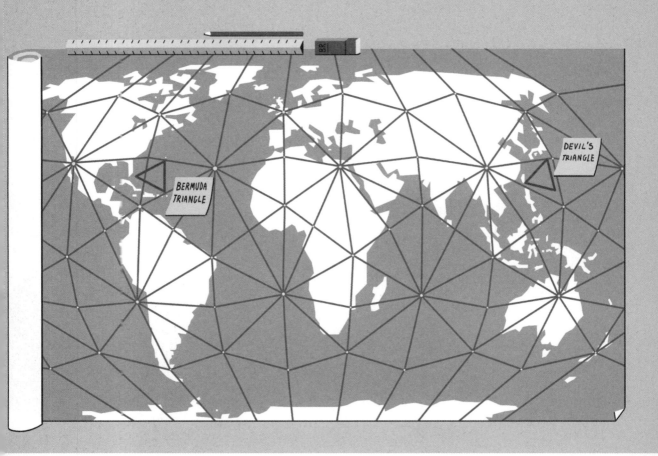

VILE VORTICES

According to some paranormal experts, strange phenomena that can be plotted on a map to reveal special hotspots.

Ley Lines

In the 1920s, British amateur archaeologist Alfred Watkins theorised that ancient landmarks were deliberately aligned. Watkins called the connections leys (from the old English for clearing). Though rejected by many experts at the time, the theory was popular with paranormal enthusiasts in the 1960s. They believed ley lines were full of magic, causing hauntings and attracting UFOs.

Bermuda Triangle

This loose zone in the North Atlantic Ocean is known for its many strange disappearances. Most famously in 1945, the US Navy's *Flight 19*, composed of five planes all disappeared at the same time. According to some adherents to the theory, the Bermuda Triangle is one of the largest haunted areas in the world or is plagued by aliens.

Devil's Sea

This oceanic triangle is found south of Japan and has been host to several ship disappearances. Authors writing on the subject have defined the triangle's size and shape differently. Critics believe the legend was largely invented by American paranormal author Charles Berlitz.

PHANTOM ANIMALS

Some ghosts have been witnessed to take an animal-like form. Cryptozoology (the study of paranormal creatures) label examples as cryptids, though the distinction between ghost, monster and animal is often unclear due to the diverse cultural interpretations.

1. The Red Ghost (Eagle Creek, USA, 1883)

2. Martyn's Ape, also referred to as a monkey (UK, circa 16th Century)

3. Ghost Deer (Mt. Eddy, USA, 20th Century)

4. Old Martin (UK, 1816)

5. Nightmare (Europe, 13th Century)

6. Alien Big Cat (UK, 20th Century)

7. Phantom Dog (Leeds Castle, UK, 19th Century)

8. Black Shuck (UK, 16th Century)

9. Black Cat (Oxenby, UK, 19th Century)

10. Cherry the Dog (Tapiola, Finland, 1974)

11. Gef The Talking Mongoose (Isle of Man, UK, 1931)

12. Materialised Guinea Pig (UK, 19th Century)

13. Ghost Goose (Melonsby, UK, circa 19th Century)

14. Ghost Owl (Eastern Russia, 19th Century)

The Exorcism of Loch Ness

Some cryptozoologists believe the Loch Ness Monster is an ancient creature that miraculously survived extinction. However, in 1975, an English Vicar attempted to exorcise the reputed beast, believing it to be an evil spirit which psychically caused alcoholism and depression in the local area.

HAUNTED INSTITUTIONS

Island of Poveglia
Venice, Italy, Circa 1960s

The island of Poveglia in the Venetian lagoon was converted into a quarantine island in the 18th century. Quarantined for over 100 years, many bubonic plague victims were left for dead, and their bodies were burned or buried en masse here. In 1922, the island's buildings were converted into an asylum for the mentally ill until closure and later abandonment in the 60s.

In 2016, five American tourists were rescued from the island after their ghost hunt was abandoned in fright. Their visit was likely inspired by a 2009 episode of *Ghost Adventures*, centred on the island. The Italian sceptic organisation CICAP judged that the island had few local associations with ghosts until it became subject of TV and blogs.

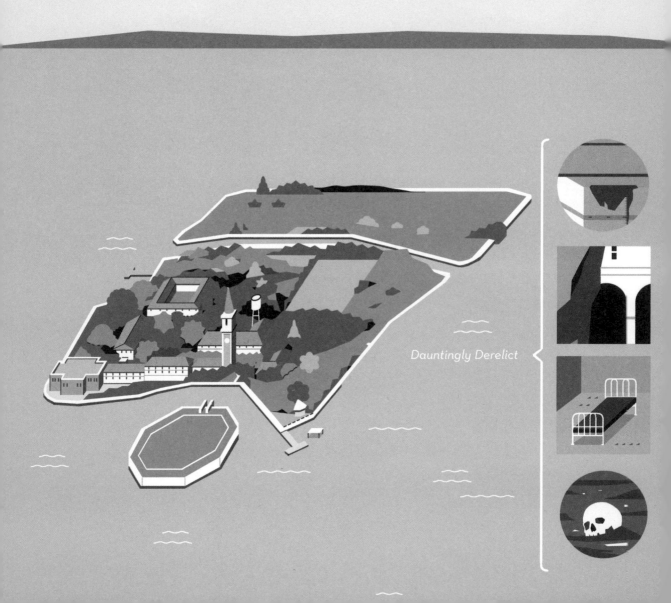

Dauntingly Derelict

Horror in Heels

Madam Koi Koi is a ghost legend believed to originate in Nigeria. The ghost is said to haunt boarding schools, where she prowls around bathroom stalls and frightens students in their beds. Her name, Koi Koi, is an onomatopoeia, alluding to the clacking of her heels.

It is believed the story originated in Nigeria's Federal Schools during the 1960s. The legend affirms that the ghost was a former teacher known for cruelty and strictness. In one telling, Madam Koi Koi was murdered by students, making her visitations a form of revenge.

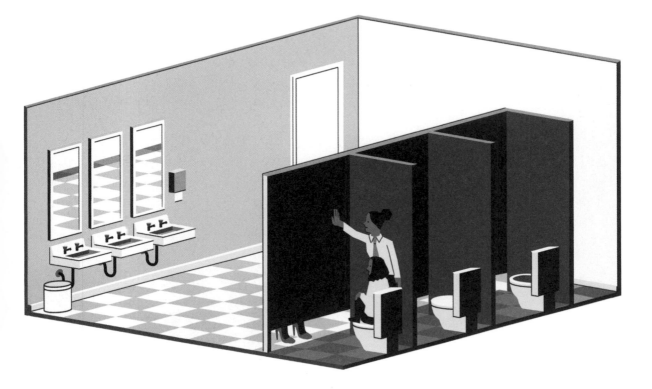

In some tellings the ghost is invisible besides its phantom footwear.

The ghost is said to menace students in their dormitories.

The ghost is said to pinch and slap students.

GHOSTS IN MEDIA

The first on-screen appearance of ghosts was in French director George Méliès's *Le Manoir du Diable* (1896). Typical of the period, the ghosts are depicted as flailing figures covered in white sheets. In the following decades, ghosts have made many appearances in film, TV and video games.

1. Banquo, *Macbeth* (1606)
2. Jacob Marley, *A Christmas Carol* (1843)
3. Ghost, *Le Manor du Diable* (1896)
4. Ghost, *Ghost Stories of an Antiquary* (1904)
5. Ghost, *The Uninvited* (1944)
6. Casper, *Casper the Friendly Ghost* (1945)
7. Oiwa, *The Ghost of Yotsuya* (1959)
8. The Man, *Carnival of Souls* (1962)
9. Ghost, *The Stone Tape* (1972)
10. Ghost Pirate, *The Fog* (1980)
11. Obi Wan, *The Empire Strikes Back* (1980)
12. Blinky, *Pac-Man* (1980)

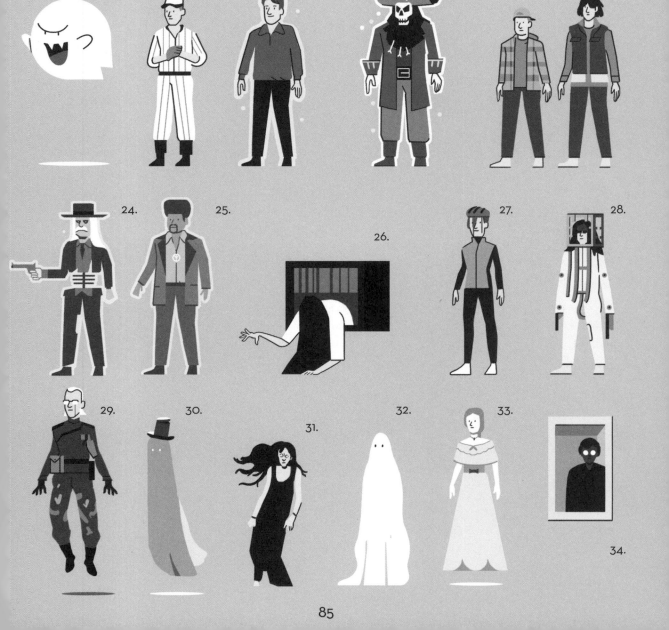

THE POSTMODERN ERA

Pacman arcade cabinet (1980)

HIGHGATE CEMETERY

During the postmodern era, the mass media platforms of television and newspapers allowed for the swift and widespread reportage of hauntings. In one case of media-enabled hysteria, the gothic Victorian Highgate Cemetery was rushed upon by paranormal enthusiasts, vandals and self-styled exorcists.

Highgate Cemetery
London, UK, 1960s

Events began in 1968 when miscreants drove an iron stake through a coffin. After witnesses saw grey apparitions prowling the cemetery, hopeful ghost hunters arrived to confront the paranormal interlopers.

Some believed the graveyard was afflicted with the presence of a vampire. One vandal even beheaded an entombed corpse and set it alight, presumably believing it to be a vampire.

Occult Rivalry
Exorcist Sean Manchester and occultist David Farrant competed to resolve the situation. Their feud was well documented in the press, drawing further crowds.

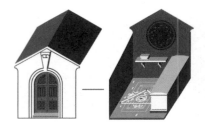

Occult markings were used in attempt to exorcise the influence of vampires and ghosts.

British Tombs with Peculiar Legends

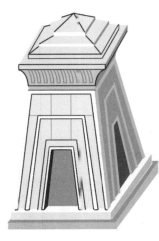

Hannah Courtoy's Tomb
Brompton

Dubiously rumoured to contain a secret teleportation machine.

William MacKenzie's Tomb
Liverpool

An Egyptian-style pyramid. MacKenzie's ghost has reportedly been seen nearby.

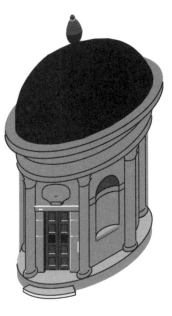

George MacKenzie's Tomb
Edinburgh

This tomb's haunted reputation grew after being repeatedly desecrated by vandals.

POSSESSED POSSESSIONS

Many legends describe the haunting of objects by an invasive ghost, demon or curse. Haunted items are typically old in nature, as though their vintage invites spirit inhabitation.

In 1952, ghost hunters Ed and Lorraine Warren opened one of the first haunted museums called The Warren Occult Museum. Built in the back of their house, the museum boasted a collection of dolls,

masks and other accursed objects. In 2017, television ghost hunter Zak Bagans opened his own museum of curios in Las Vegas. Visitors are encouraged to sign a waiver, in case they fall victim to unseen forces.

1. 0888 88888, the haunted phone number
2. *The Legendary Painting of Glamis Castle*, a window is said to light itself
3. Haunted Mirror, Myrtles Plantation, LA, USA
4. Haunted Chest, a common item in legends

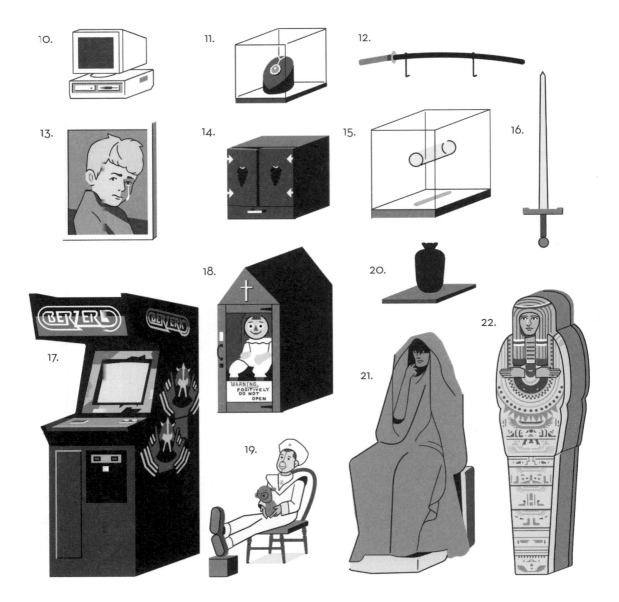

5. Haunted Phone Booth in Mizumoto Park, Japan
6. The Screaming Skull, Burton Agnes Hall, UK
7. *The Hands Resist Him*, a reputedly haunted painting by Bil Stoneham
8. Busby's Stoop Chair, Thirsk Museum, UK
9. La Pascualita, the mannequin, Chihuahua, Mexico
10. Haunted Amstad PC1512, Stockport, UK
11. The Hope Diamond, National Museum of Natural History, Washington DC, USA
12. Muramasa Swords, Japan
13. *The Crying Boy*, several paintings featuring crying children are said to be haunted

14. The Dybbuk Box, reputedly a demon trapped in a box
15. The Phantom Cylinder, the Tower of London, UK
16. Haunted Sword, many antique weapons carry legendary curses
17. Bezserk Video game Cabinet, USA
18. Annabelle Doll, Warren's Occult Museum, Monroe, CT, USA
19. Robert Doll, East Martello Museum, FL, USA
20. The Basano Vase, buried in Italy
21. Black Aggie Statue, Washington DC, USA
22. The Unlucky Mummy, The British Museum, UK

GHOST TOWNS

Abandoned settlements attract the moniker ghost town. Settlements can be abandoned for a variety of reasons, such as pressures of economy, environment and war. Ghost towns often gain the reputation for being haunted, even when few ghost experiences are recorded. The lack of people and the damage from flora and weather leave the towns lonely and unnerving spaces.

Calico Ghost Town, CA, USA
From the 1950s, this abandoned Old West mining town was marketed as a tourist destination. Restoration efforts took historical liberties by adding elaborate façades to buildings. Regular ghost tours are held to share accounts of local hauntings.

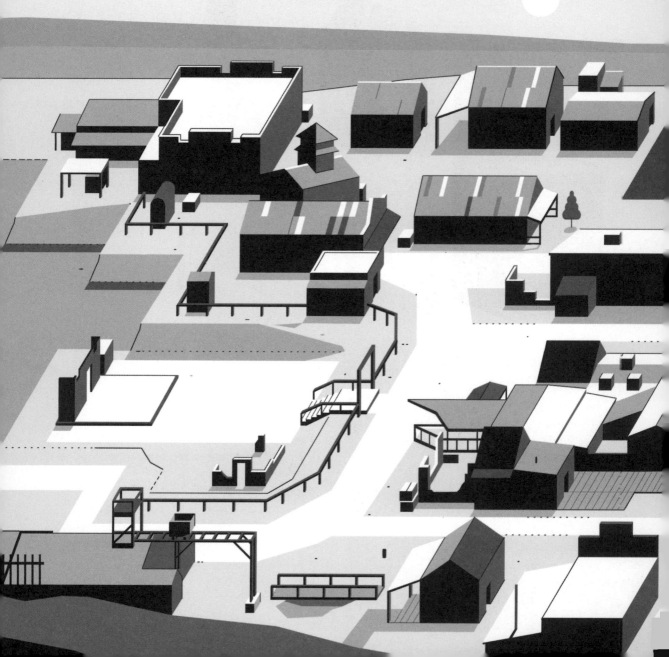

Jazirat Al Hamra, United Arab Emirates

For some centuries Jazirat Al Hamra was home to a small pearling fleet but was largely abandoned in 1968 after inhabitants moved to larger settlements. Despite rumours of Jinn, the abandoned town has since been used as an outdoor art gallery.

Sanzhi UFO houses, Taiwan

A collection of incomplete prefabricated houses. Construction was halted in 1980 after financial issues. The site attracted a haunted reputation following nearby fatal road incidents and deaths by suicide. According to some, the houses were built on a Dutch burial ground. The site was demolished in 2010.

THE WHITE LADY

One of the most common ghost legends is the *White Lady*, so called due to her flowing white clothing. Some social critics believe white lady legends were used to affirm patriarchal parables on women. The legends usually describe the ghost's tragic end as being related to their perceived failings as wives or mothers.

La Llorona

Common in Latin America are tales of *La Llorona* (Spanish for the wailer), who drowned her own children, then herself after being betrayed by her Spanish conquistador lover. Some believe the legend precedes European colonisation, however the most common tellings depict the ghost as a local woman who haunts bodies of water.

Y Ladi Wen

A Celtic legend found in Wales, *Y Ladi Wen* (Welsh for white lady) is a ghost believed to perform various functions. In some areas, she is thought to guard cauldrons filled with treasure, while other tales place her as a desperate wandering spirit that cries out for help.

HELPWCH FI!

Witte Wieven

Mythology in the Netherlands and Belgium describe the ghost apparitions of *Witte Wieven* (Dutch for wise, or white women). Their roles in myths are much like witches or færie, as they practice medicine, trickery and are made agreeable with offerings.

Naale Ba

A ghost found that plagued rural communities in the 1990s. It was believed this ghost knocked on people's doors and imitated voices to gain entry. Those who answered the ghost's knocks were thought to vanish mysteriously the next day. Homeowners were led to write *Naale Ba* (meaning come tomorrow in Kannada language) on their doors to thwart the ghost.

Kaperosa

Kaperosa ghosts may be found in the Philippines. They are generally believed to be harmless and are strongly tied to the place of their deaths.

AMITYVILLE HAUNTING

Amityville

Long Island, NY, USA, 1975

In 1975, 23-year-old Ronnie DeFeo Jr confessed to murdering six of his family members in their home. Shortly after, George and Kathy Lutz and their three children moved into the very same house. Concerned about potential ghosts, the Lutzes' invited a priest to bless the house. Soon however, the family noted a plethora of paranormal events.

Some of the reported Haunted Happenings

| 'Pig' seen only by children | Cloven footprints | Invisible grasping hands | Phantom music | Slamming doors | Mirror apparitions |

DeFeo's lawyer convinced the Lutzes' to hold a press conference about the haunting. After many interviews the Lutzes' became tired of ridicule and chose writer Jay Anson to pen a book. The book, *The Amityville Horror: A True Story* (1977) featured some creative embellishment, including flies and bleeding walls.

When the Lutzes moved out, they invited an ensemble of paranormal researchers to scrutinise the property. Investigators included famous ghost hunters Hans Holzer and Ed and Lorraine Warren. The first film adaptation *The Amityville Horror* (1979) was followed by many sequels and spinoffs.

Exorcism met with phantom voices

Ghost Hunter frenzy

GHOST PHOTOS

Unlike 19th century studio-based spirit photography, ghost photography is taken at reportedly haunted locations. Ghost photos are taken on lightweight cameras, camcorders and CCTV. Like UFO photography, they often feature blurry and indistinct shapes. This uncertainty invites excited speculation when they are circulated in media.

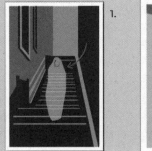

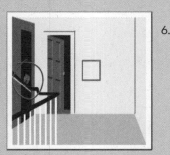

1. **Raynham Hall, UK, 1936**
   Reputed photo of The Brown Lady ghost. Sceptics believe it to be an example of double-exposure trickery.

2. **Borley Rectory, UK, 1944**
   Reputed evidence of a ghost-thrown brick, possibly thrown by a worker off-camera.

3. **Ipswich, UK, 1959**
   Apparent photo of a ghost car passenger. Sceptics again suggest the probability of double exposure.

4. **London, UK, 1966**
   Ghost aficionado Peter Underwood sent this photo to Kodak. After analysis, they found no obvious evidence of tampering.

5. **Worsted Church, UK, 1975**
   An apparent luminescent ghost seated on a pew. The effect could have been achieved with overexposure.

6. **Amityville, NY, USA 1976**
   A reputed photo of a ghost boy taken during paranormal investigations. Sceptics believe the subject to simply be one of the investigators, taken by surprise.

7. **Saint-Jean-de-Maurienne, France, 1950s**
   Documentation of poltergeist activity. The objects may simply have been thrown by a person off-camera.

8. **Texas, USA, date unknown**
   An upside down shadow figure. Some believe the photo was a digital invention made in the 2000s.

SATANIC PANIC

Interest in ghosts and séances has faced opposition by those who fear such activities incite the Devil. Most famously, a moral panic spread in North America from the 1970s, during which believers claimed secret Satanic worshipers worked in high places of government, media and institutions.

Films such as *The Exorcist* (1973) encouraged a growing fear and suspicion with Ouija boards. The popular role-playing game *Dungeons and Dragons* was also believed to be dangerous and was compared to devil worship.

Reputed possession symptoms

Loss of appetite

Unusual strength

Paranormal feats

Exorcism

Exorcism is the ritualistic attempt to remove a spirit from a person or place. According to myth and legend, possessed people exhibit a range of symptoms from a loss of appetite to unusual strength. Famously, the Christian Bible described Jesus performing an exorcism on a man possessed by a demon called Legion.

In Catholicism, the rite of exorcism has been practiced for centuries. The rite largely fell out of favour until the 1970s during the heights of Satanic Panic.

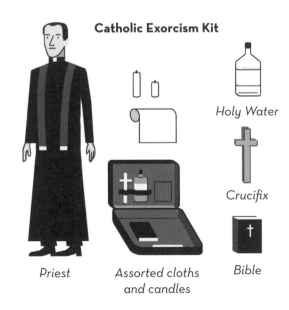

Catholic Exorcism Kit

Priest

Assorted cloths and candles

Holy Water

Crucifix

Bible

GHOST HUNTERS IN MEDIA

Literature and screen depictions of ghost hunters are varied, from heroic spiritual warriors to glib entrepreneurs. Most famously, the film *Ghostbusters* (1984), pitted jumpsuit-wearing scientists against ghosts and inter-dimensional demons.

The Gateway of the Monster (1910)
1. Thomas Carnacki

The Haunting of Hill House (1959)
2. Dr. John Montague

Scooby-Doo Where Are You? (1996)
3. Scooby-Doo
4. Shaggy Roggers
5. Velma Dinkley
6. Daphne Blake
7. Fred Jones
8. The Mystery Machine

The Ghost Busters (1975)
9. Kong
10. Eddie Spencer
11. Tracy

Pac-Man (1980)
12. Pac-Man

Poltergeist (1982)
13. Dr. Martha Lesh
14. Dr. Ryan Mitchell

Ghostbusters (1984)
15. Proton Pack
16. Ray Stantz
17. Winston Zeddemore
18. Peter Venkman
19. Egon Spengler
20. Janine Melnitz
21. Ghost Trap
22. Ecto-1

Dirk Gently's Holistic Detective Agency (1987)
23. Dirk Gently

The X-Files (1993)
24. Dana Scully
25. Fox Mulder

Mona the Vampire (1999)
26. Mona

Luigi's Mansion (2001)
27. Luigi

Wellington Paranormal (2018)
28. Sergeant Ruawai Maaka
29. Officer O'Leary

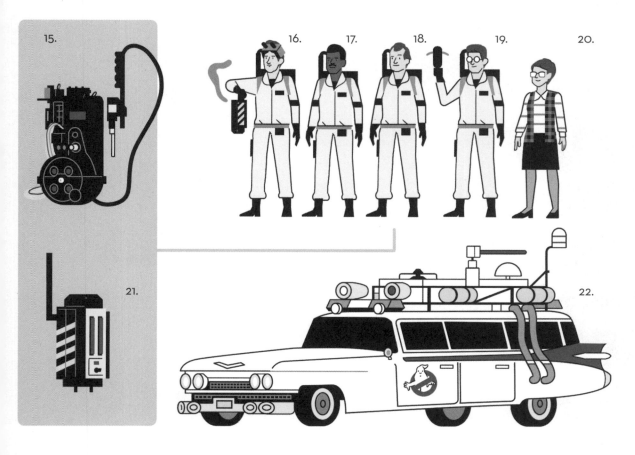

THE 21st CENTURY

Online ghost video (circa 2019)

TV GHOST HUNTING

From the beginning of the 21st century, reality television greatly influenced the culture of ghost hunting.

Chiefly an American product, ghost TV shows star predominantly white men, who mix investigations with theatrics. Episodes are heavily edited with music and sound effects to heighten drama and thrills.

Ghost hunter Harry Price was the first to broadcast a live ghost hunt on BBC radio in 1936. The popularity of the TV series *The X-Files* (1993) catalysed a plethora of paranormal themed shows that emerged in the 21st century.

Presenters

Production crew

Most Haunted (2002–Present)
British show *Most Haunted* broadcast ghost hunts, set against playful lighting and dry ice. The show was also influential in its use of utilitarian wardrobes and the starring of spirit mediums.

Ghost Hunters (2004–Present)
Ghost Hunters follows the The Atlantic Paranormal Society's (TAPS) investigations of reportedly haunted locations. The show features the crew brandishing a dazzling array of instruments which they believe to evidence the presence of ghosts.

Ghost Adventures (2008–Present)

Ghost Adventures follows American ghost hunter Zak Bagans and team during ghost hunts. The format involves team members brandishing electrical equipment and emoting at strange noises. The series has spawned successful spin offs and the Zak Bagans Haunted Museum in Las Vegas.

Example TV Ghost Hunting Crew

Executive Producers	Researcher	Sound Recordist
Hosts/Investigators	Production Coordinator	Postproduction Supervisor
Editors	Assistant Editors	Legal Council
Writers	Music	Co-Producer
Producer	Second Camera	Production Accountant
Line Producer	Online Editor	Equipment Tech
Director of Photography	Audio Mixer	Still Photography
Production Manager	Graphic Designer	Local PA's

MODERN HAUNTINGS

Sherman Ranch
UT, USA

Sherman Ranch has reputedly attracted a plethora of unusual events, including ghosts, UFOs and cryptids. In 1996, businessman Robert Bigelow commissioned researchers to study any signs of paranormal. After two decades of inconclusive study, the site repeatedly changed ownership. Today the real estate is marketed as Skinwalker Ranch, appropriating a creature from Navajo mythology.

Spirit and Simulacra
Despite inconclusive evidence, the rumours of paranormal activity here has made the ranch subject to documentaries, a loose fictional adaptation and merchandise.

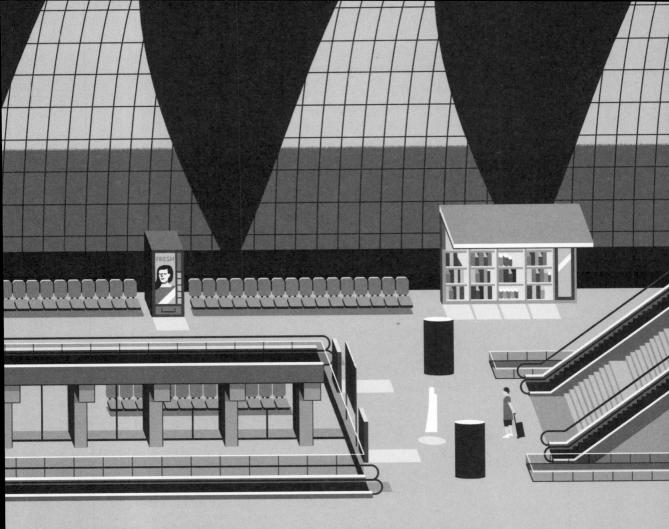

Suvarnabhumi Airport
Bangkok, Thailand

Since its development in 2006, the Suvarnabhumi airport has acquired
a haunted reputation due to its reputed location above an ancient burial
ground. During construction, contractors experienced phantom wailing and
strange incidents. Events climaxed with the arrival of 99 Buddhist monks,
who led a nine-week long exorcism ritual. During the final hours, one man
appeared to become possessed by a blue-faced ghost who called himself
Poo Ming, the guardian of the buried cemetery.

HAUNTED HOTELS

Hotels are a common site for reputed hauntings, due to legendary deaths of guests and staff. Some establishments, such as the Jamaica Inn in England, freely advertise their hauntings as an amenity. Reputedly haunted hotel rooms may even be priced differently due to high demand.

Jamaica Inn, Cornwall, England

First World Hotel
Genting Highlands, Pahang, Malaysia

Despite only being constructed in 2001, the First World Hotel in Malaysia offers a good few ghost legends. One story involves ghosts repeatedly falling from high windows, reenacting their final acts in life. Many stories derive from internet forums and amateur ghost hunters on YouTube, the latter being torch-wielding enthusiasts creeping around dark corridors and parking lots.

Mizpah Hotel, Nevada, USA

INTERNET GHOSTS

In the early days of the internet, people shared ghost legends in email chains and on forums. Sharing features on 21st century social media has made it easier to distribute legends to a wider audience.

Many internet ghost legends started as horror fiction, and typically included a digitally altered creepy image. Wide proliferation meant stories lost their original context, and many were soon considered genuine accounts of the strange. Contemporary critics refer to this category of legend as 'digital folklore'.

SPCG
A reputedly haunted image, shared in early email chains.

Ben Drowned
A multi-media project, which posed as a genuine account about a haunted video game.

Click Bait
The internet is full of content engineered to generate views and revenue. Reputedly real ghost photos and videos are common clickbait fodder.

Kunekune
Users have shared reputedly genuine encounters with the ghost Kunekune, which started as fiction on Japanese forums.

ENDURING LEGENDS

Many of the hauntings in this book are bound to a specific locus (such as a building or period of time). Yet, some ghost legends are found all over the world with new sightings or tellings reported to this day.

Phantom Hitchhiker

The phantom hitchhiker is a common urban legend that came to prominence in the 20th century. In the 1940s, folklorists Richard Beardsley and Rosalie Hankey collected over 70 unique versions of the ghost story.

The legend was largely popularised by writer Jan Brunvand's book *The Vanishing Hitchhiker* (1981), which provided a scholarly analysis.

In most common accounts, charitable drivers collect the hitchhiker at night. The passenger acts oddly and disappears during the journey with a dramatic flair. Later, the confused driver interviews locals and discovers their passenger was a ghost.

Bloody Mary

One of the better-known ghosts Bloody Mary originated as a form of fortune telling, called catoptromancy (from the Greek for mirror divination). Traditionally, Bloody Mary is evoked during ritual, wherein the participant stares into a mirror, lit only by a candle. Upon incantation of "Bloody Mary … Bloody Mary … Bloody Mary!" An apparition is supposed to manifest, either of a future romantic partner or as the titular ghost of Mary, covered in blood.

While catoptromancy has likely existed for as long as we've had polished surfaces, the exact origin of the Bloody Mary ghost is unclear, although in the UK she is commonly associated with Queen Mary the First.

GHOSTS THROUGH TIME

1. Silbón Ghost, Venezuela
2. Nurse Ghosts, Cambridge, UK
3. Blackbeard's Ghost, Ocracoke, USA
4. Yakshi, India
5. Submarine Lieutenant, Atlantic Ocean
6. RAF Pilot, Croydon, UK
7. The Headless Horseman, Europe
8. Krahang, Thailand
9. Trapper Ghost, Labrador, Canada
10. Limping Woman, Pyecombe, UK
11. Black Knight, Fort Manoel, Malta
12. Myling, Scandinavia
13. Nang Takian, Thailand
14. Knights of Ålleberg, Sweden
15. Pharaoh, Valley of Kings, Egypt

16. Gwisin, Korea
17. Mae Nak, Thailand
18. Hitodama, Japan
19. Mononoke, Japan
20. Preta, Thailand
21. Wraith, UK
22. Pocong, Indonesia

23. Ma Phae Wah, Myanmar
24. Phonegyi Thaye, Myanmar
25. The Headless Nun, Canada
26. Shirime, Japan
27. The Sandown Clown, Isle of Wight, UK
28. Spadebeard, Great Dismal Swamp, USA
29. Viking, York, UK

GHOSTS TODAY

Nowadays, one can still hear ghost stories from friends, family, books and the news. Do you, reader, have a tale to tell?

Ghosts are central to religious festivals, reminding us to honour the dead and beware the dark. They dwell in the depths of fiction to horrify and delight, appearing in prose, cinema and video games. While scientific explanations expand, many still enjoy the thrill of a shared chilling story. If you are brave enough to look for you own ghosts, then do so responsibly! The trespassing of a dark, derelict building holds dangers far more profound than a shrieking ghost.

At the very least, the power of ghosts is to inspire thrill and fear, leaving us to reach for a light with nervous hands.

I hope you will join me in asking the eternal question;

Is anyone there?

PEOPLE OF GHOSTLORE

1. Joseph Glanvill (ghost hunter)
2. Catherine Crowe (writer)
3. Maggie Fox (manager)
4. Kate Fox (medium)
5. Leah Fox (medium)
6. Helena Blavatsky (theosophist)
7. W.F. Taylor (spiritualist)
8. Allan Kardec (spiritualist)
9. Arthur Conan Doyle (writer, spiritualist)

10. Harry Houdini (magician, debunker)
11. Bess Houdini (magician, debunker)
12. Rose Mackenberg (debunker)
13. Rukmini Devi Arundale (dancer, theosophist)
14. Paschal B. Randolph (spiritualist)
15. P.T. Barnum (showman)
16. Cora L.V. Scott (medium)
17. Eleanor Sidgwick (psychical researcher)

18. Henry Sidgwick (psychical researcher)
19. Aleister Crowley (occultist)
20. Charles Fort (writer)
21. William Marriott (magician, debunker)
22. Leafy Anderson (medium)
23. Daniel Dunglas Home (medium)
24. Harry Price (ghost hunter)
25. Rudi Schneider (medium)
26. Elijah Bond (Ouija inventor)
27. Wassily Kandinsky (artist, spiritualist)

GLOSSARY

Afterlife
A religious concept referring to the residence of souls after death.

Apport
The appearance of objects out of thin air.

Astral Projection
The claimed ability of individuals to separate their soul and body.

Doppelgänger
The paranormal double of a living person, often seen as a bad omen.

Ectoplasm
A substance regurgitated by mediums during the communication with spirits.

Exorcism
The dismissal of spirits by a religious leader, such as a Catholic priest.

Electronic Voice Phenomena (EVP)
The apparent recordings of ghostly voices on recording devices.

Extra Sensory Perception (ESP)
The reception of information through paranormal means; this may include telepathy or clairvoyance.

Ghost Hunter
Investigators of hauntings, typically with the intent to provide an explanation.

Ghost Mob
The large gathering sightseers at well-reported hauntings.

Haunting
An area, person or object associated with frequent or repeated paranormal activity.

High Strangeness
A term coined by Ufologist J. Allen Hynek, referring to peculiar details from UFO cases. Often applied to other areas of the paranormal.

Necromancy
The conjuring of the dead through magic.

Mass Hysteria
A group panic based on fear, producing collective illusions and obsessive behaviour.

Medium
An individual with the alleged ability to communicate with the spirits of the dead.

Near-Death Experience (NDE)
Visions seen by people in life-threatening situations. Experiences often involve a bright light.

Occult
The broad study of magic, mysticism and the paranormal.

Pareidolia
Recognising patterns in random data – for example, a menacing figure in a shadow.

Possession
In which an individual, object or animal is inhabited by a malevolent entity.

Psychic
An individual who claims to infer knowledge through paranormal means.

Psi
Abbreviation of psychic phenomena.

Séance
The French for 'session'; a formalised meeting between a medium and spirits.

Sceptic
An individual that values scientific inquiry and methodology.

Sleep Paralysis
An experience in which people awake unable to move. Often accompanied with hallucinations and the feeling of being weighed down.

Soul
The concept that living things contain a spirit.

Stone Tape
The theory that psychic energy can be stored by the environment, objects and buildings.

Telepathy
The psychic transmission of thoughts.

Trigger Object
Some ghost hunters plant objects at suspected hauntings in attempt to provoke ghosts.

Woo
The use of scientific-sounding words to support fringe theory. 'Woo' is also a sound ghosts make.

Reputedly haunted New Amsterdam Theatre, USA

FURTHER READING

 CROWE, Catherine, (1847), *The Night Side of Nature*. Reprint, London, UK: British Library, 2010

 MICHEAL, John & RICKARD, Robert, (1977), *Phenomena: A Book of Wonders*. London, UK: Thames and Hudson

 BESSANT, Annie, LEADBEATER, Charles W, (1901), *Thought Forms*. Reprint, New York, USA: Sacred Bones Books, 2020

 BLUNDELL, Nigel & BOAR, Roger, (1983), *The World's Greatest Ghosts*. London, UK: Octopus Books Ltd

 JAMES, M.R., (1904), *Ghost Stories of an Antiquary*. Reprint, New York, USA: Dover Publications, 2011 (Fiction)

 ADAMS, Douglas (1987), *Dirk Gently's Holistic Detective Agency*. New York, USA: Simon & Schuster

 JACKSON, Shirley, (1959), *The Haunting of Hill House*. Reprint, London, UK: Penguin Classics, 2014 (Fiction)

 CHASE, Robert David, et all (1989), *Ghost Hunters*. New York, USA: St. Martin's Press

 VALLÉE, Jacques, (1969), *Passport to Magonia*. Reprint, Brisbane Australia: Daily Grail Publishing, 2014

 SPENCER, John & Anne, (1992), *The Encyclopedia of Ghosts & Spirits*. London, UK: Headline Book Publishing

 GREEN, Andrew, (1973), Ghost Hunting: A Practical Guide. Reprint, Suffolk, UK: Arima Publishing, 2016

 RANDLES, Jenny, (1994), *The Afterlife*. New York, NY, USA: Berkley Books

 MAYNARD, Christopher, (1977), *The World of the Unknown: Ghosts*. Reprint, London, England, Usborne 2019

 MICHEALS, Susan, (1996), *Sightings*. New York, NY, USA: Fireside

RANDLES, Jenny, (1996) *The Paranormal Source Book*. London, UK: Piatkus

 HOLZER, Hans, (1997), *Ghosts: True Encounters With The World Beyond*. New York, USA: Black Dog & Leventhal

 SLEMAN, Thomas, (1998), *Strange But True*. London, UK: London Bridge

 CLARKE, Roger, (2012), A *Natural History of Ghosts: 500 Years of Hunting for Proof*. Reprint, London UK: Penguin Books Ltd

 RUICKBIE, Leo, (2013), *Ghost Hunting*. London, UK: Constable & Robinson Ltd

 COVERLY, Merlin, (2020), *Hauntology*. Harpenden, UK: Oldcastle Books Ltd

 FINKEL, Irving, (2021), *The First Ghosts*. London, UK: Hodder & Stoughton

FURTHER VIEWING

Night of the Demon (1957),
dir. Jacques Tourneur [Film],
Columbia Pictures

House (1977),
dir. Nobuhiko Obayashi [Film],
Toho

The Innocents (1961),
dir. Jack Clayton [Film],
20th Century Fox

The Evil Dead (1981),
dir. Sam Raimi [Film],
New Line Cinema

Carnival of Souls (1962),
dir. Herk Harvey [Film],
Herts-Lion International

The Shining (1980),
dir. Stanley Kubrick [Film],
Warner Bros.

The Haunting (1963),
dir. Robert Wise [Film],
Metro-Goldwyn-Mayer

Poltergeist (1982),
dir. Tobe Hooper [Film],
Metro-Goldwyn-Mayer

Scooby Doo, Where Are You?
(1969), dir. Joseph Barbera
& William Hanna [TV],
Taft Broadcasting

Ghostbusters (1984),
dir. Ivan Reitman [Film],
Columbia Pictures

The Stone Tape (1972),
dir. Peter Sasdy [TV], BBC2

Beetlejuice (1988),
dir. Tim Burton [Film],
Warner Bros.

The Exorcist (1973),
dir. William Friedkin [Film],
Warner Brothers

The Exorcist III (1990),
dir. William Peter Blatty [Film],
20th Century Fox

The Frighteners (1996),
dir. Peter Jackson [Film],
Universal Pictures

 The Others (2001),
dir. Alejandro Amenábar [Film],
Warner Bros.

 Coco (2017),
dir. Lee Unkrich [Film],
Walt Disney Studios

 Ghost Stories (2017),
dir. Jeremy Dyson [Film],
Lions Gate

 The Haunting of Hill House (2018),
dir. Mike Flanagan [Series], Netflix

 Ghosts (2019), dir. Tom Kingsley
[TV], BBC One

 The Haunting of Bly Manor (2020),
dir. Mike Flanagan [Series], Netflix

INDEX

ELEANOR SIDGWICK

SOCIETY FOR PSYCHICAL RESEARCH
Est. 1882

YES OUIJA NO
ABCDEFGHIJKLM
NOPQRSTUVWXYZ OU
1234567890
GOOD BYE

WORLD OF THE LIVING ← | ↑ SUMMERLAND

THE BEREAVED ↓ | THE STRANGERS

'I SPOKE TO YOU BY THE GLASS'

MATER HAN

'TABLE TIPPING'

STAGECRAFT

TABLE MOVING,

A

↑↑↓↓←→←→ B A

SPIRIT CABINET

MAGIC

APPORT

MANIFEST -ATION

ZENNER CARDS

BORLEY RECTORY

33

ST AUGUSTINE LIGHTHOUSE

SÉANCE ROBE